The Human Body: Organs and Functions

LIVER

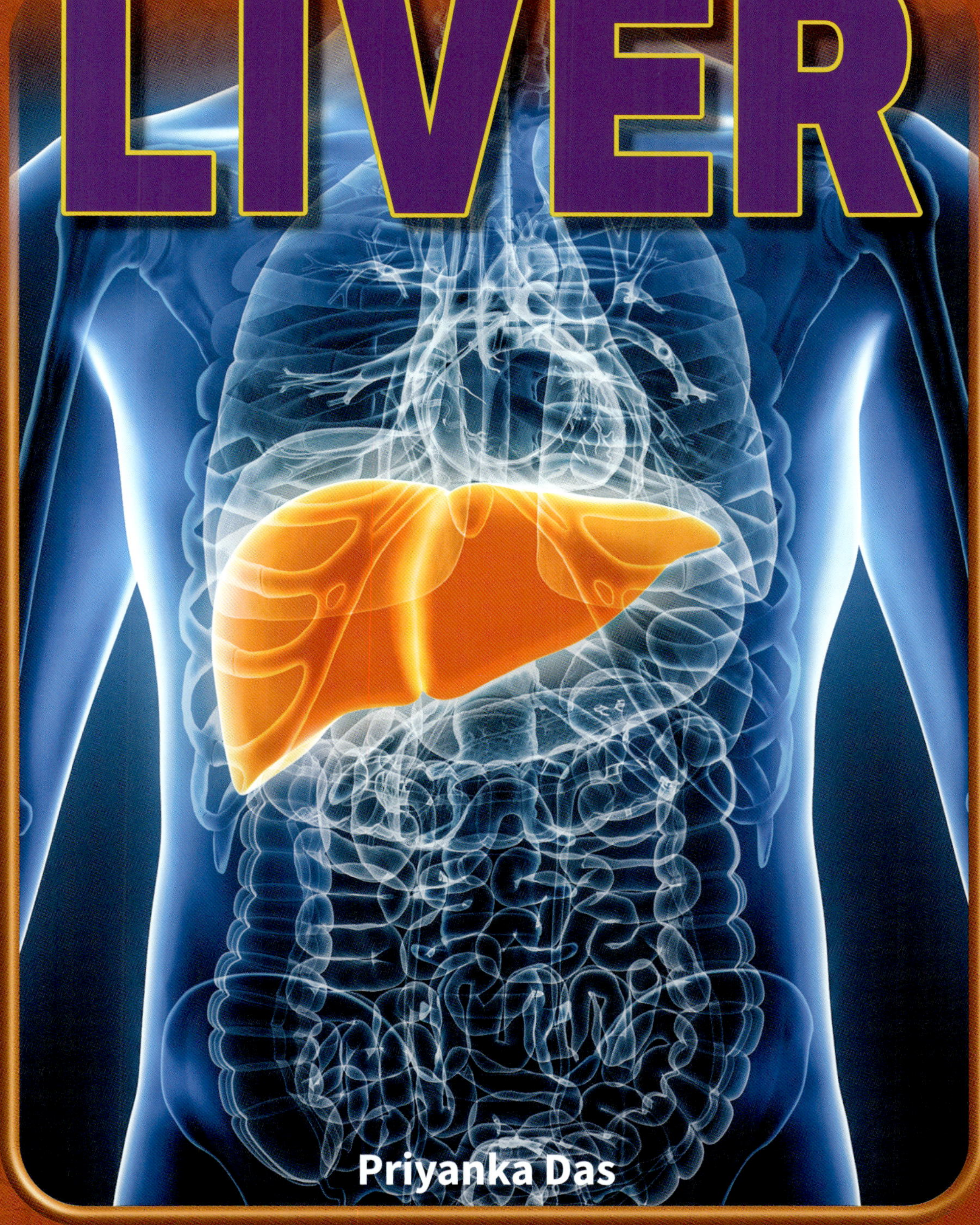

Priyanka Das

LIGHTBOX
openlightbox.com

LIGHTBOX

Go to **www.openlightbox.com** and enter this book's unique code.

ACCESS CODE

LBXD5932

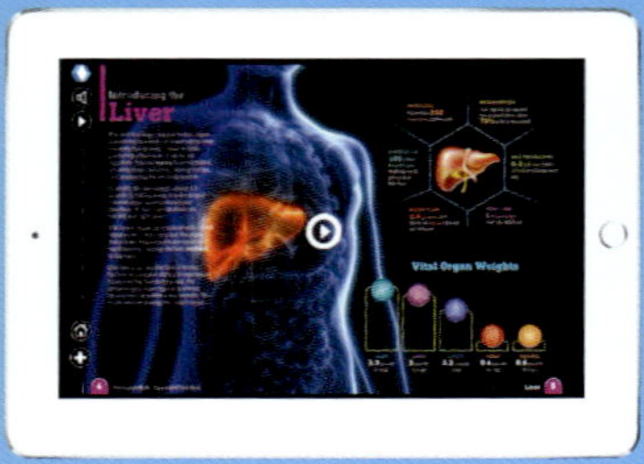

Lightbox is an all-inclusive digital solution for the teaching and learning of curriculum topics in an original, groundbreaking way. Lightbox is based on National Curriculum Standards.

LIGHTBOX SUPPLEMENTARY RESOURCES

SHARE
Share titles within your Learning Management System (LMS) or Library Circulation System

CURRICULUM
Find national and state curriculum correlations

CITATION
Create bibliographical references following APA, CMOS, and MLA styles

STANDARD FEATURES OF LIGHTBOX

AUDIO High-quality narration using text-to-speech system

ACTIVITIES Printable PDFs that can be emailed and graded

SLIDESHOWS Pictorial overviews of key concepts

VIDEOS Embedded high-definition video clips

WEBLINKS Curated links to external, child-safe resources

TRANSPARENCIES Step-by-step layering of maps, diagrams, charts, and timelines

INTERACTIVE MAPS Interactive maps and aerial satellite imagery

QUIZZES Ten multiple-choice questions that are automatically graded and emailed for teacher assessment

KEY WORDS Matching key concepts to their definitions

This title is part of our Lightbox digital subscription

Lightbox Grades 6–8 Subscription
ISBN 978-1-5105-6068-0

Access hundreds of Lightbox titles with our digital subscription. Sign up for a **FREE** subscription trial at **www.openlightbox.com/trial**

The digital components of this book are guaranteed to stay active for at least five years from the date of publication.

The Human Body: Organs and Functions

LIVER

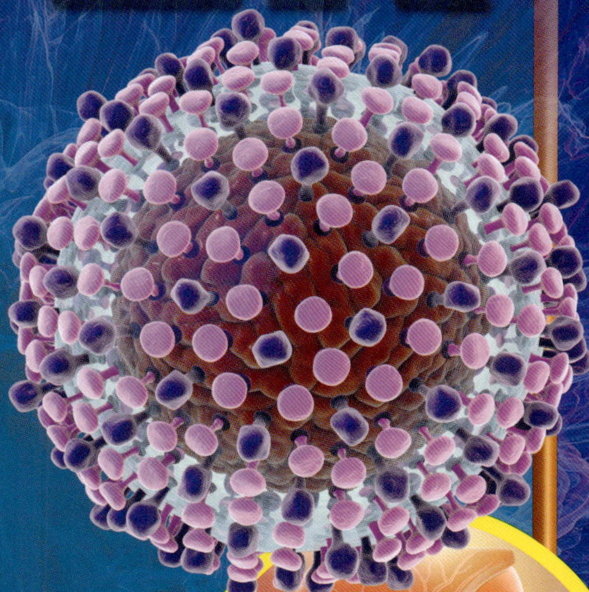

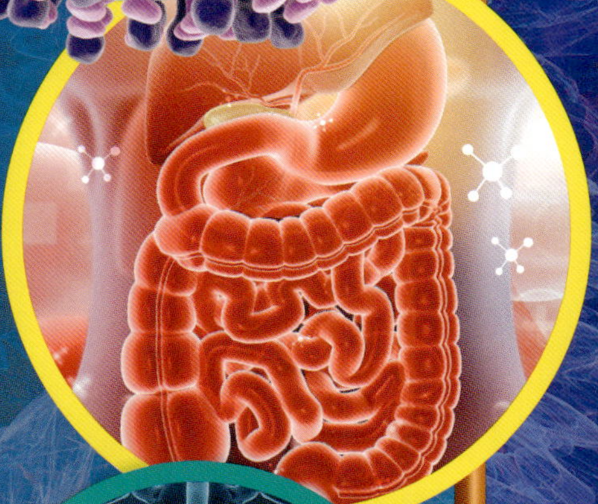

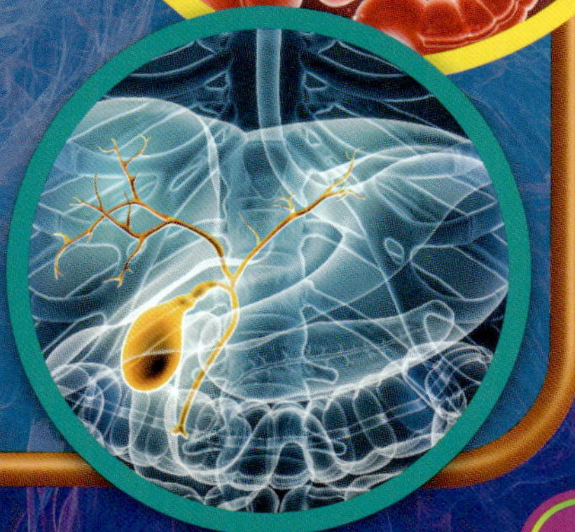

CONTENTS

Introducing the Liver

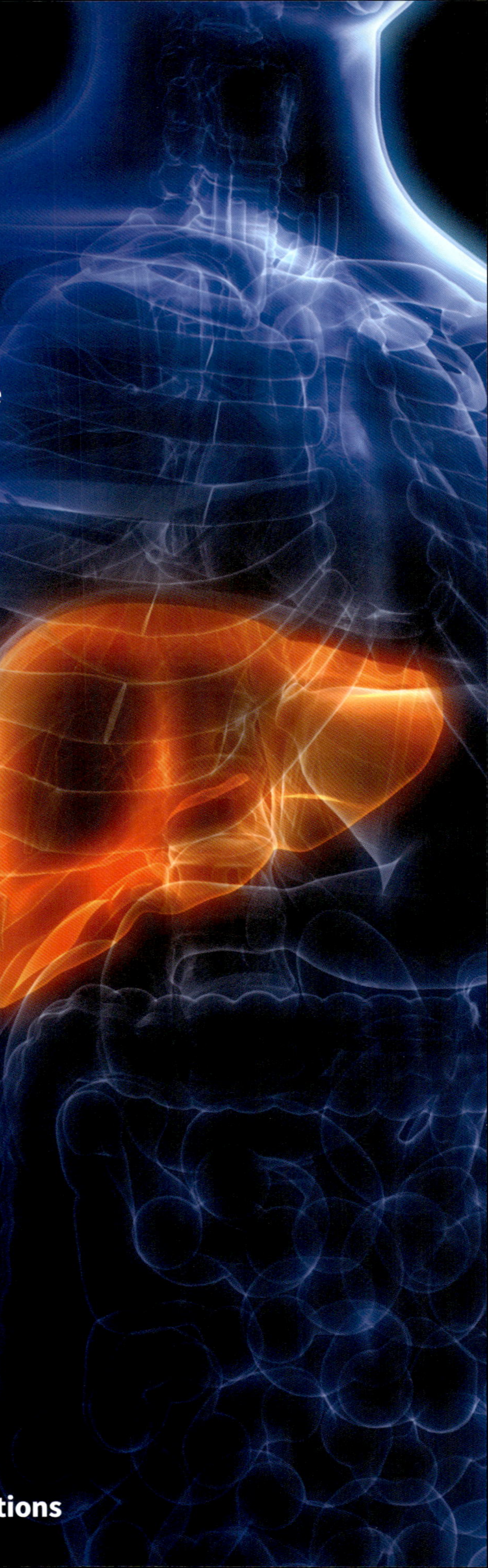

The liver is a large, reddish-brown **organ**. It performs hundreds of processes to keep the human body functioning. One of these is producing bile, a greenish-yellow **digestive** fluid. Other tasks include filtering **toxins**, breaking down **nutrients**, and storing energy.

In adults, the liver weighs about 3.3 pounds (1.5 kilograms). It is the largest internal organ and has a complex structure. Its two main sections are its left and right lobes.

The liver is made up of **cells** called hepatocytes. They carry out the organ's many tasks. Hepatocytes heal rapidly, making the liver resilient to damage.

One characteristic the liver is known for is its remarkable ability to regenerate. If some of the liver is removed, the remaining part can regrow to almost its original size within a few months. This is uncommon among human organs.

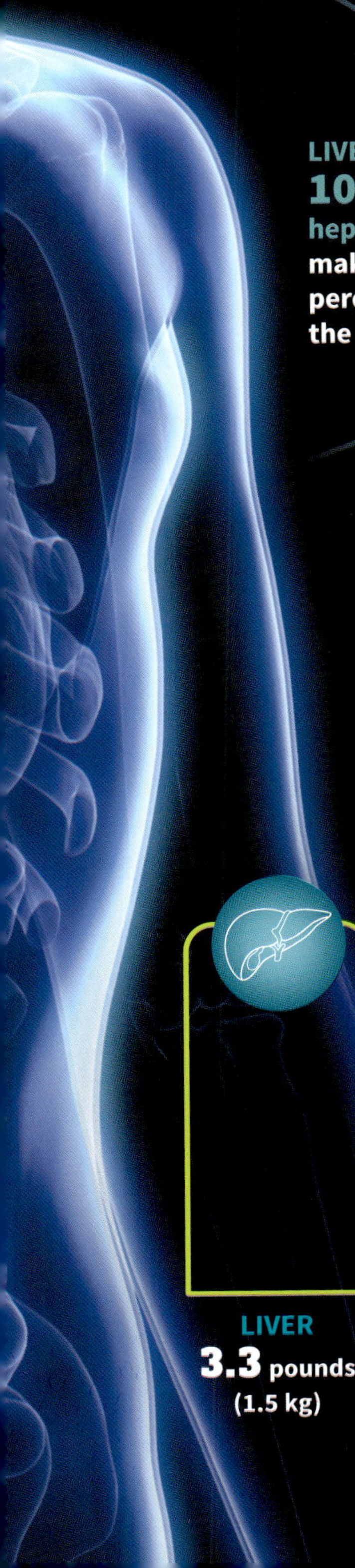

PROCESSES
Performs more than **500 functions**

REGENERATION
Can regrow to normal size even if more than **75 percent** of it is removed

LIVER CELLS
100 billion hepatocytes make up 80 percent of the liver

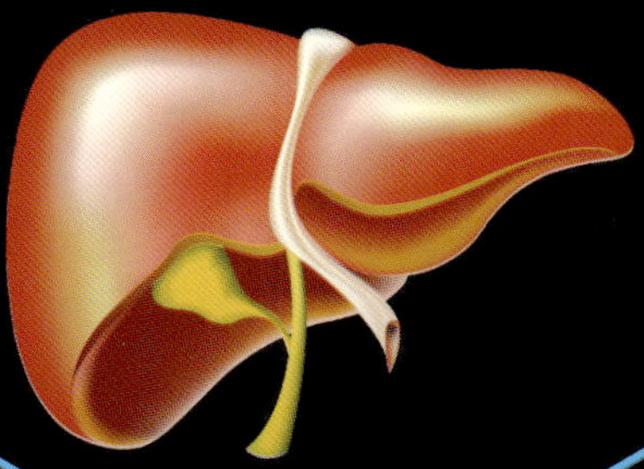

BILE PRODUCTION
Produces **0.2 gallons** (0.8 L) of **bile** each day

BLOOD FLOW
Filters **0.4 gallons** (1.5 liters) of **blood** per minute

RIGHT LOBE
6 times larger than the left lobe

Vital Organ Weights

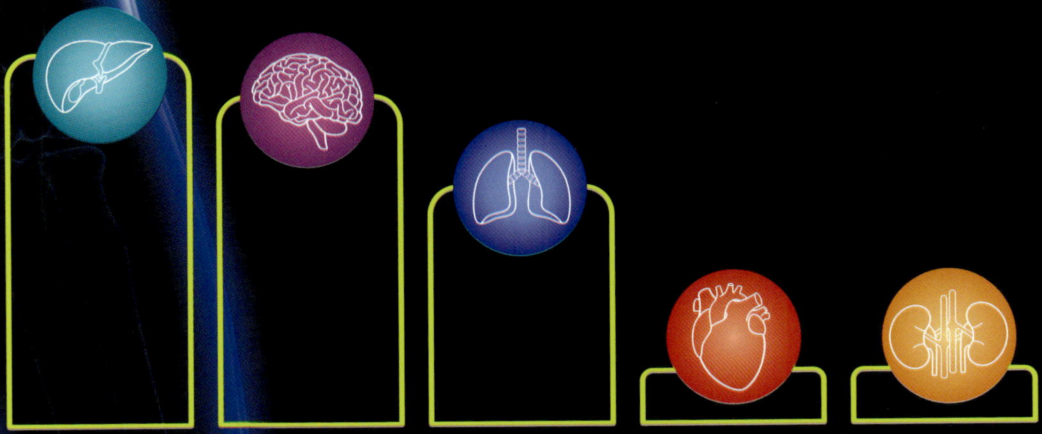

LIVER	BRAIN	LUNGS	HEART	KIDNEYS
3.3 pounds (1.5 kg)	**3** pounds (1.4 kg)	**2.2** pounds (1 kg)	**0.6** pounds (0.3 kg)	**0.5** pounds (0.2 kg)

The Body's Organ Systems

There are 78 organs in the human body. Many work together to perform related tasks and are grouped in categories called organ systems. All of a person's activities and bodily functions are made possible by 11 main organ systems working together.

The liver is primarily part of the digestive system. This system is responsible for turning food into nutrients that the body can use. The bile that the liver produces breaks down fats in the **small intestine**. Several other organ systems have a close connection to the liver as well.

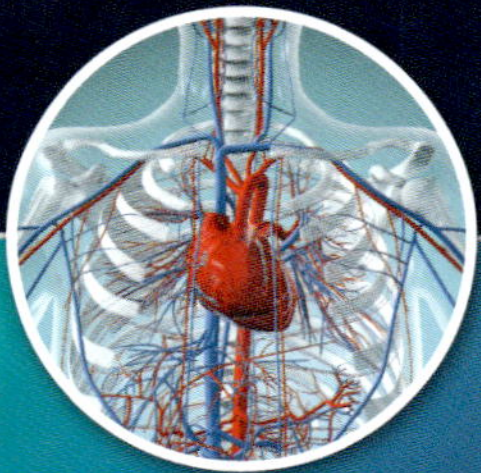

Circulatory System
Transports blood, moving substances to and from the body's cells

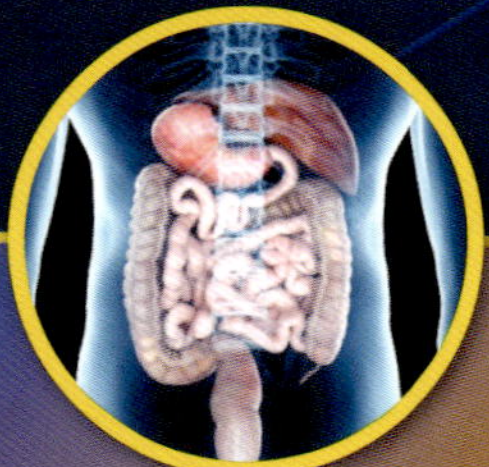

Digestive System
Extracts energy and nutrients from food

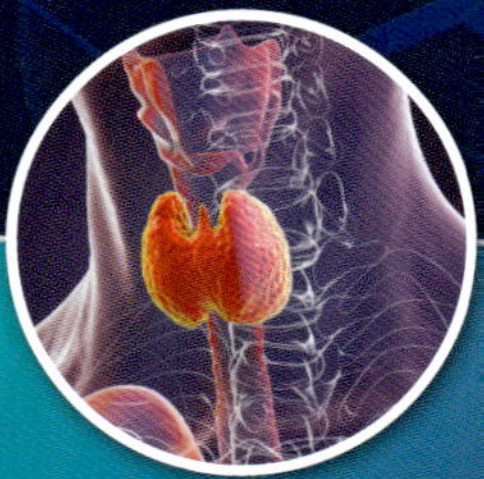

Endocrine System
Controls the release of **hormones** and maintains **homeostasis**

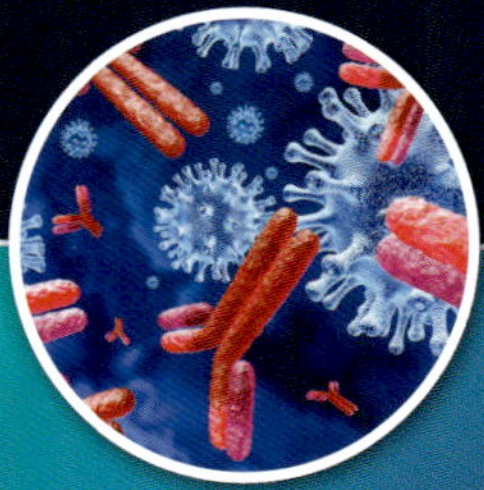

Immune System
Protects the body from attack by **pathogens**

Integumentary System
Protects the internal organs and is primarily made up of skin

Muscular System
Works together with the skeletal system to allow the body to move

The circulatory system transports blood throughout the body. It relies on the liver to filter out toxins from the blood. The liver also helps the endocrine system regulate blood sugar by storing **glucose** in a form called glycogen. The sugar is released when it is needed by the body. This maintains steady blood sugar levels. The liver also helps remove excess hormones from the body.

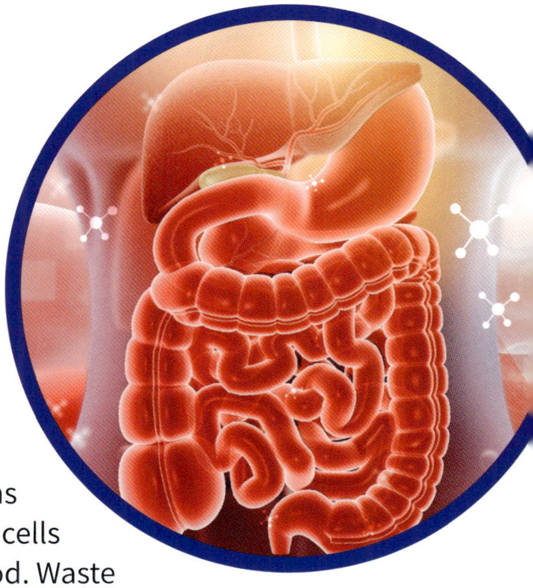

The liver plays a role in the immune and urinary systems as well. Special immune cells in the liver called Kupffer cells help filter pathogens and damaged cells out of the blood. Waste products processed in the liver are sent to the intestines as bile or filtered by the kidneys for removal in urine.

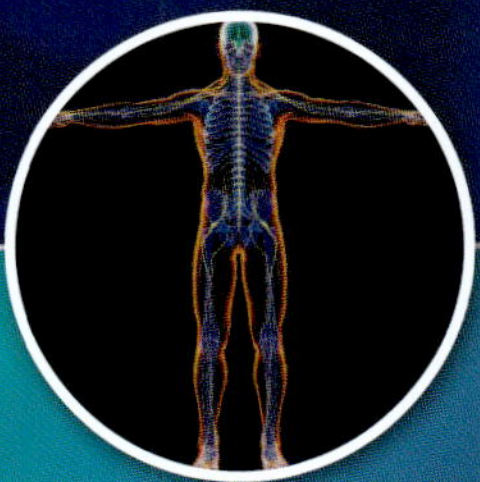

Nervous System
Carries signals between the brain and the rest of the body

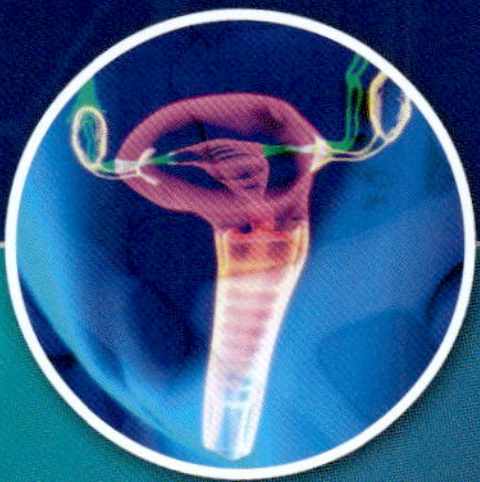

Reproductive System
Enables people to have children

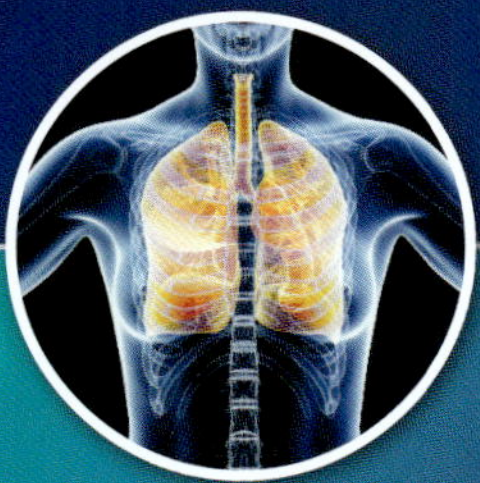

Respiratory System
Removes carbon dioxide from the body and takes in oxygen

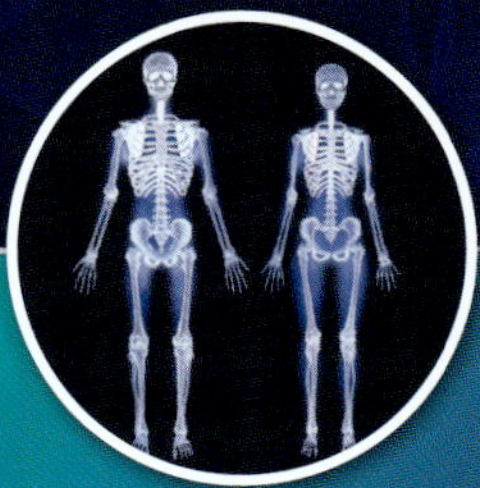

Skeletal System
Supports the body and protects the internal organs

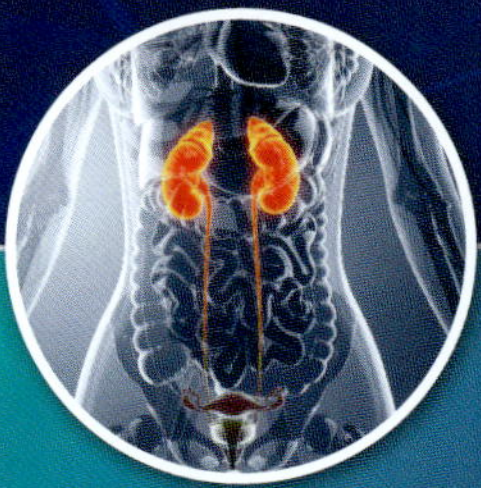

Urinary System
Filters blood, removing excess water and some waste products

Structure of the Liver

Located in the upper right **abdomen**, the liver is below the diaphragm and above the stomach, right kidney, and intestines. The gallbladder is nestled just under it. In addition to its main right and left lobes, the liver has two smaller lobes known as the caudate lobe and quadrate lobe. These are attached to the right lobe.

These four **hepatic** lobes are made up of small masses of tissue called lobules, which appear hexagonal when viewed under a microscope. Each lobule contains rows of hepatocytes arranged in a honeycomb pattern. Lobules also have a structure called a portal triad at each corner. A portal triad is made up of three tubes. These are branches of the hepatic artery, hepatic portal vein, and bile duct.

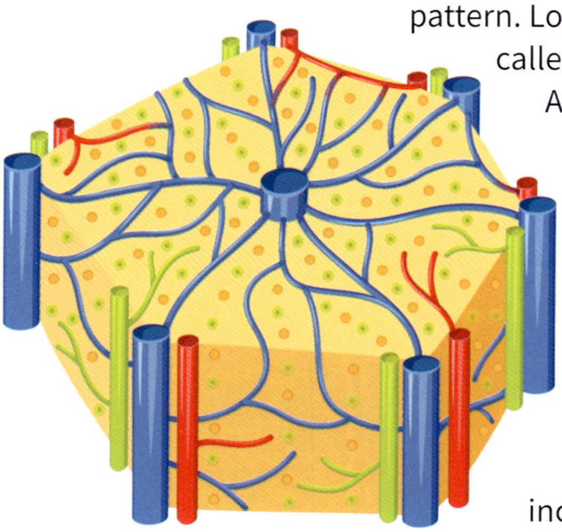

The liver's bile ducts transport bile from the liver to the gallbladder for storage. Blood vessels, including the hepatic artery and portal vein, help the liver filter blood and process nutrients. The hepatic artery carries oxygen-rich blood from the heart to the liver, while the portal vein delivers nutrient-rich blood from the digestive organs. After blood flows through the liver, it exits through a vein called the hepatic vein, which carries this filtered blood back to the heart.

Liver and Gallbladder Anatomy

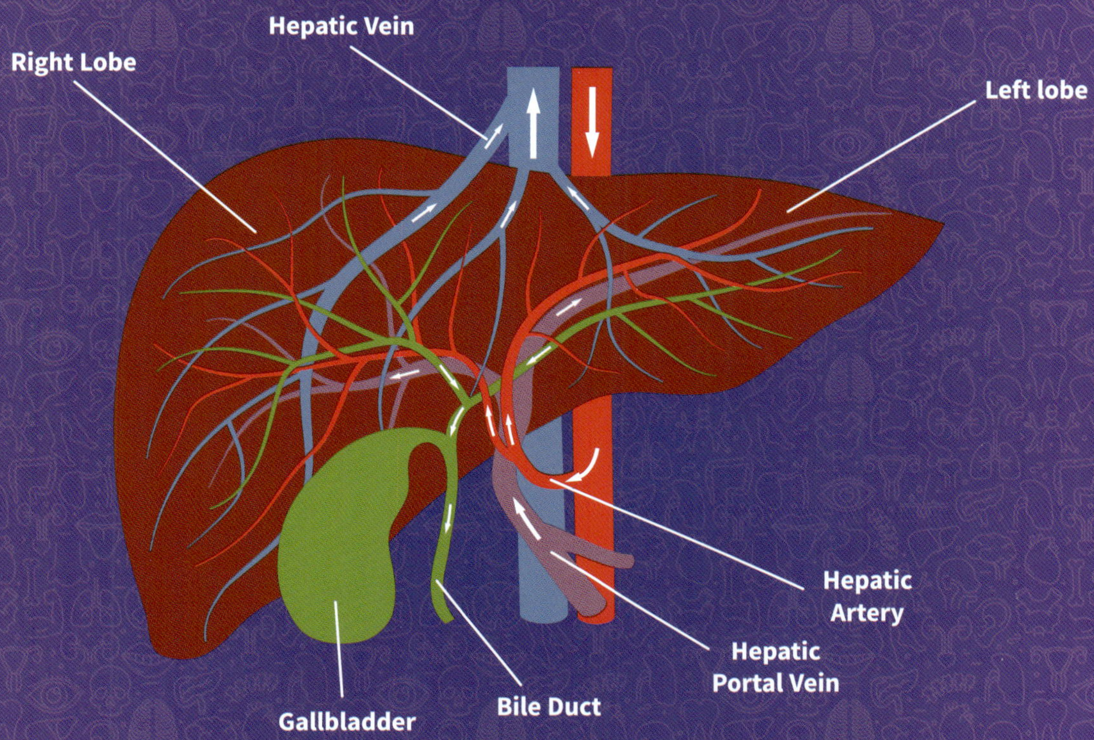

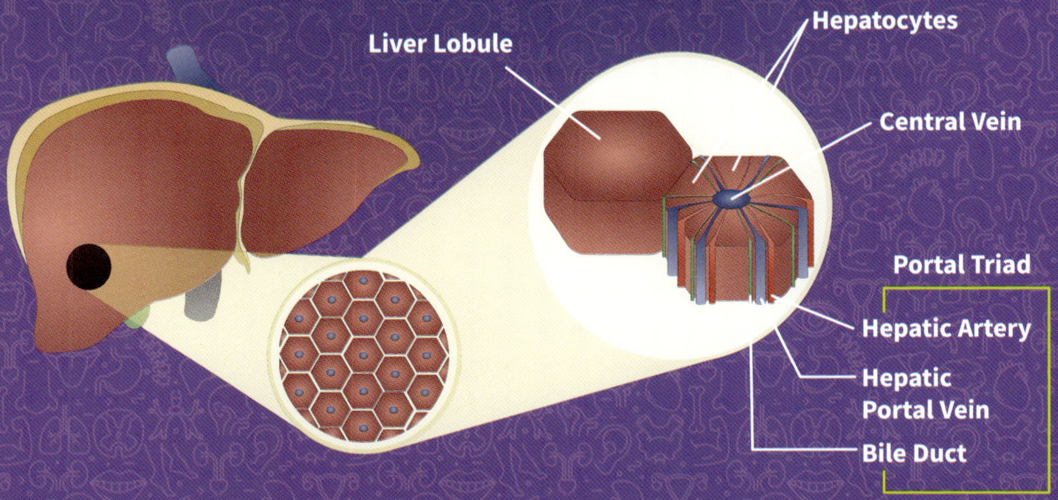

Role in the Body

The liver is an incredibly versatile organ. It processes everything that enters the body. The numerous functions that the liver performs help keep multiple organ systems working.

Detoxification

Toxins may enter the body through food, drink, medication, or the environment. The liver removes them from the blood and breaks them down into harmless substances. This process is called detoxification.

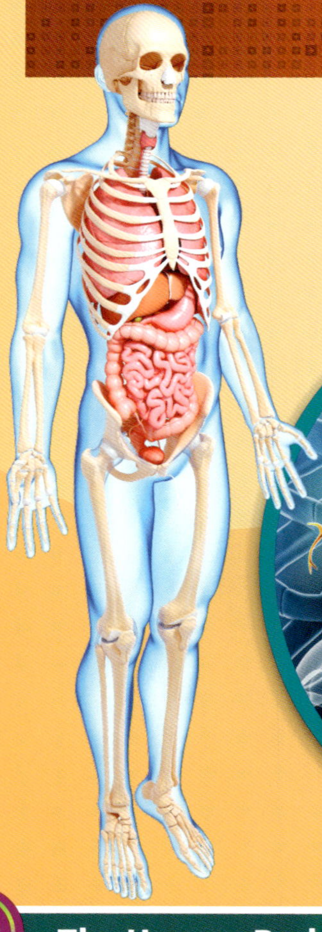

Bile Production

The body cannot absorb fats directly. However, it can absorb **fatty acids**. Bile helps with this. After being produced by the liver and transported to the gallbladder, bile remains in the gallbladder until it is needed. When food reaches the small intestine, bile is released to help break down fats into fatty acids.

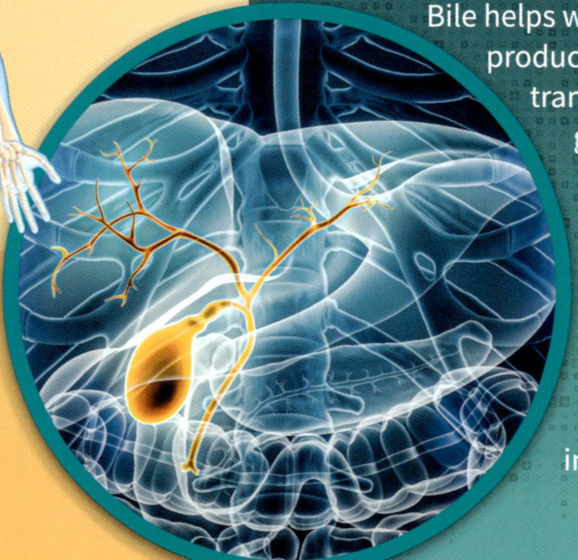

Blood Filtration

As blood flows through the liver, it is filtered to remove waste products and impurities. The liver also processes nutrients and other substances from the blood. This ensures that only healthy components circulate through the body.

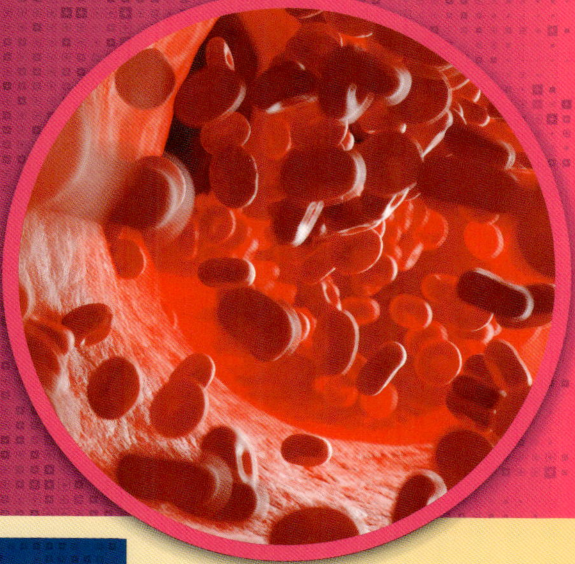

Metabolism

The liver plays a key role in metabolism. This is the breaking down of **carbohydrates**, fats, and **proteins** into forms the body can use for energy. The liver also breaks down its glycogen stores into glucose when the body needs a boost of energy.

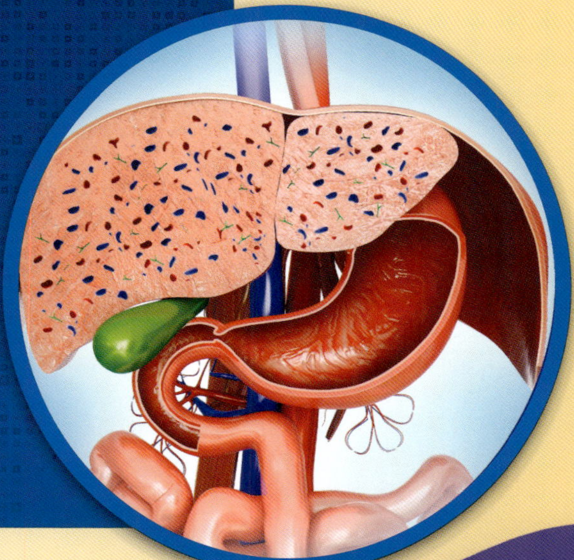

Can You Live Without It? NO!

There are five organs in the human body that are considered vital, or necessary for life. These are the brain, heart, lungs, kidneys, and liver. Without the liver, the body would not be able to process nutrients, filter toxins, or produce bile. Toxic compounds would quickly build up. Severe health complications would occur, leading to eventual organ failure. The liver's ability to regenerate makes it possible to survive when the liver is partially damaged. However, in the case of complete liver failure, a liver **transplant** is needed.

A Medical Timeline

Studying the liver has led to significant medical advances over the centuries. Today, doctors can treat liver diseases far more easily than ever before. The branch of medicine that focuses on the liver and conditions related to it is known as hepatology, coming from the Greek words *hepar*, or "liver," and *logia*, or "study."

circa 2000 BC

Priests in Mesopotamia make **clay models of animal livers**. Other early civilizations, including Babylon and ancient Egypt, document liver anatomy around this time. Some consider the organ the "seat of the soul."

circa 400 BC

In ancient Greece, the renowned physician **Hippocrates** suggests that the liver is the source of bile.

circa 200 BC

Greek physician and philosopher **Galen** describes the liver as the main organ of the human body. He believes it produces and transports blood.

1628 AD

English physician **William Harvey** studies the structure of the liver. He describes how several diseases affect the organ's appearance.

circa 1850

French scientist **Claude Bernard** researches the liver's role in converting glucose into glycogen. This reveals how the liver stores and releases energy.

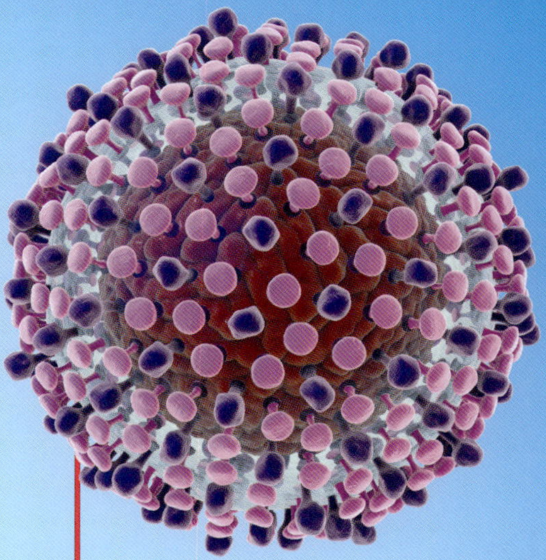

1967

In the United States, **Dr. Thomas Starzl** performs the first successful human liver transplant.

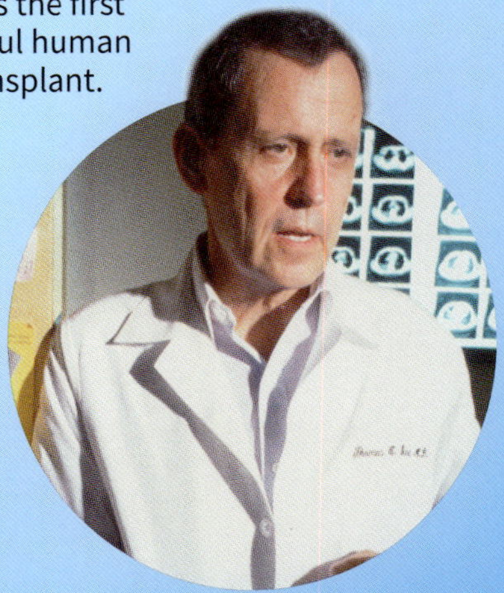

1989

The **hepatitis C virus** is discovered. This virus infects the liver, causing swelling and damage.

2013

New **medications for hepatitis C** are developed. These significantly improve treatment outcomes for patients around the world.

2020

Harvey J. Alter, Michael Houghton, and Charles M. Rice receive the **Nobel Prize** in Physiology or Medicine for the discovery of the hepatitis C virus.

2025

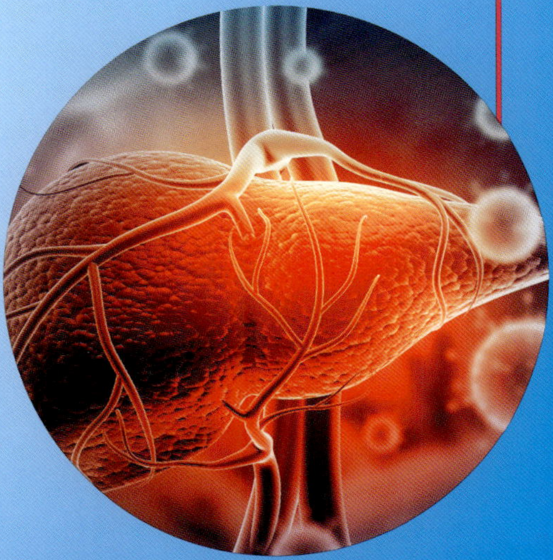

Advanced **imaging techniques** enable doctors to detect liver diseases earlier and monitor liver health with greater accuracy. Scientists work to develop devices, including artificial liver support systems, to support patients awaiting transplants.

Organs Working Together

In its role helping different body systems, the liver works closely with a number of key organs. These include the gallbladder, pancreas, kidneys, intestines, and heart. Together, these organs make sure different processes are carried out smoothly.

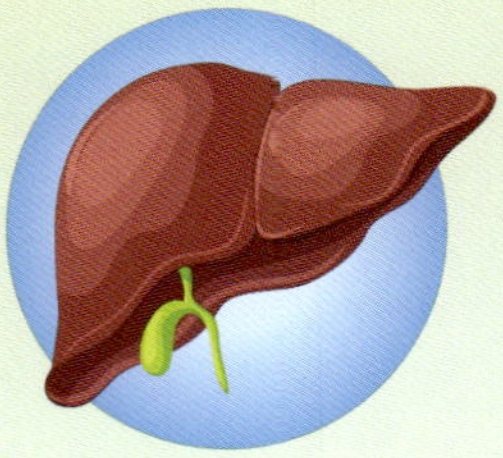

The Liver works with the...

Gallbladder to Digest Fats

Liver produces bile → Bile is stored in gallbladder → Gallbladder releases bile into small intestine → Bile helps break down fats for absorption by the body

Pancreas to Regulate Blood Sugar

Blood sugar is high → Pancreas releases a hormone called insulin → Insulin tells liver to store excess glucose as glycogen

Blood sugar is low → Pancreas releases a hormone called glucagon → Glucagon tells liver to convert glycogen back to glucose

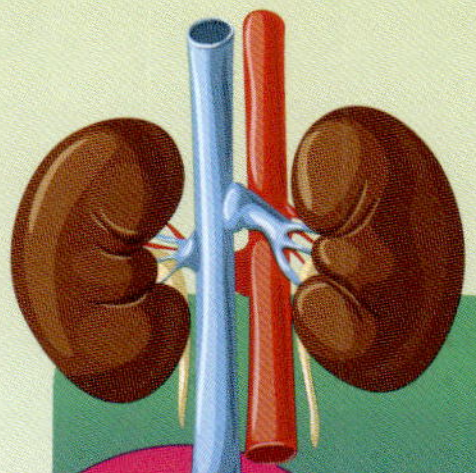

Kidneys to Filter and Excrete Waste

1. Liver breaks down toxins in blood
2. Waste products are sent to kidneys
3. Kidneys filter waste products into urine
4. Urine is excreted from body

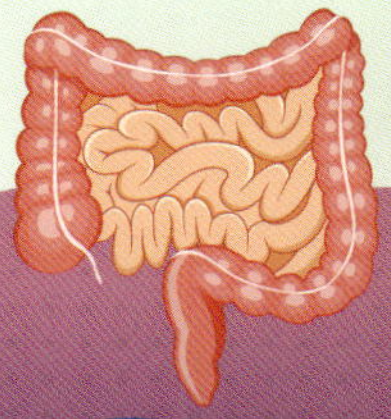

Intestines to Process Nutrients

1. Nutrients are absorbed from food in intestines
2. Nutrients enter liver through hepatic portal vein
3. Liver processes and stores nutrients
4. Processed nutrients are released into bloodstream as needed

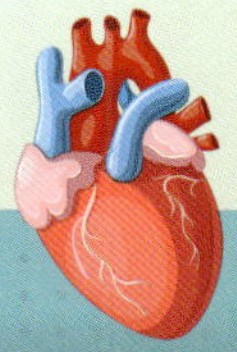

Heart to Filter Blood

1. Heart pumps oxygenated blood to liver through hepatic artery
2. Liver uses oxygen and nutrients to carry out metabolic functions
3. Liver filters blood
4. Filtered blood returns to heart via hepatic vein

Diseases of the Liver

When the liver stops functioning properly, health issues arise. Liver diseases include hepatitis, cirrhosis, fatty liver disease, and liver cancer. These can lead to partial or total liver failure.

Hepatitis

Hepatitis is an **inflammation** of the liver. It can be caused by **autoimmune** conditions, chemicals, alcohol abuse, or **viral** infections. Hepatitis A, B, and C are the most common forms of viral hepatitis. Hepatitis can damage the liver over time. If untreated, it may cause chronic, or long-term, liver disease.

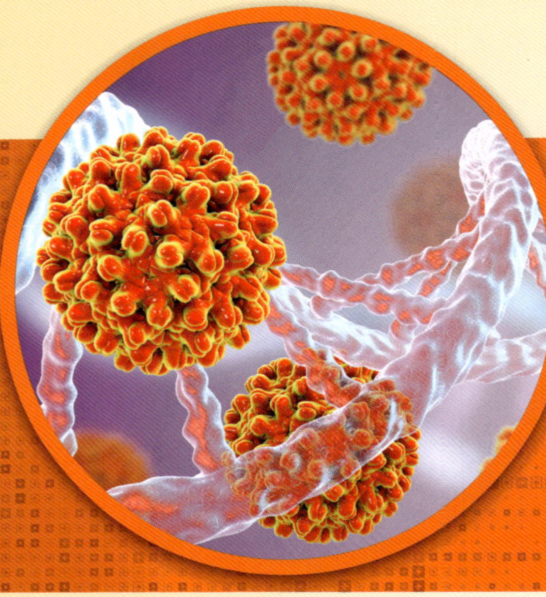

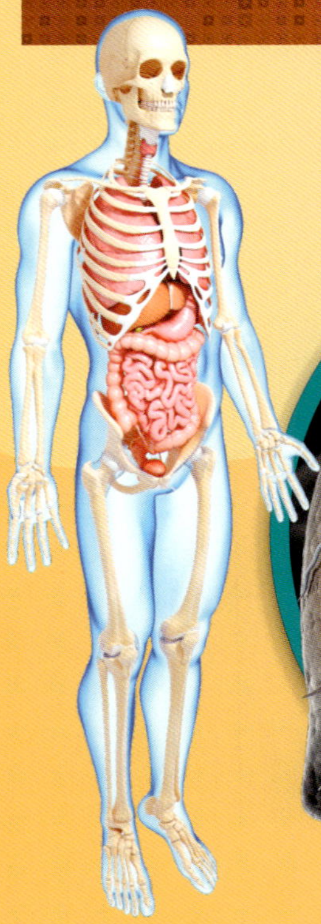

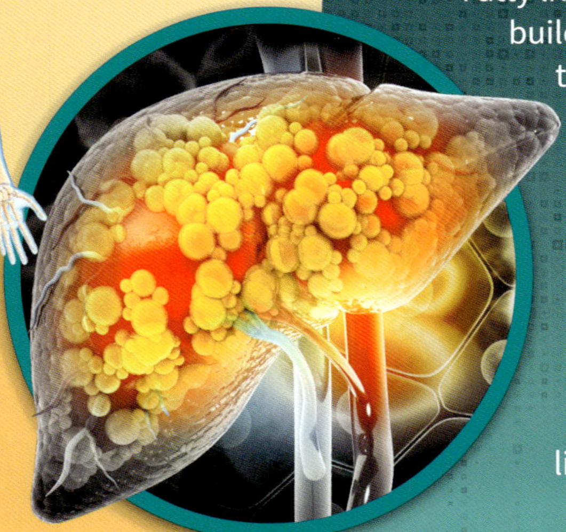

Fatty Liver Disease

Fatty liver disease occurs when fat builds up in the liver. When this is caused by excessive alcohol use, it is known as alcoholic fatty liver disease. If it is the result of a poor diet, it is called non-alcoholic fatty liver disease. Over time, this condition can lead to inflammation and liver damage.

Cirrhosis

Cirrhosis is a condition in which liver tissue becomes permanently scarred over time. This is often due to long-term alcohol use, chronic hepatitis, or other liver diseases. Scarring prevents the liver from functioning properly and can cause it to fail.

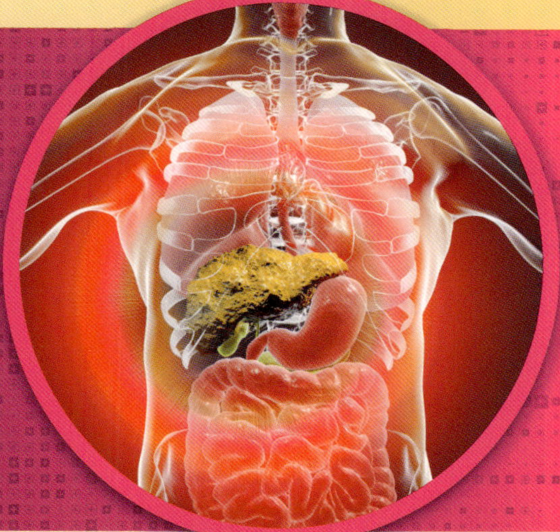

Liver Cancer

Cancer is a disease in which the body's cells reproduce and spread uncontrollably. Liver cancer occurs when these cells grow in the liver. This can develop from chronic liver diseases, such as hepatitis or cirrhosis.

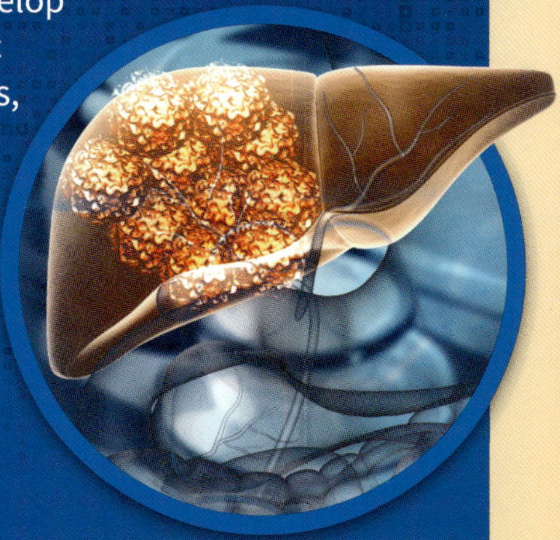

Warning Signs!

In its early stages, liver disease can be difficult to detect. However, there are some symptoms to watch out for. If these signs appear, it is important to go to a doctor right away.

- Jaundice, which is the yellowing of the skin and eyes
- Fatigue, or feeling tired and unwell
- Nausea and vomiting
- Tremors, especially trembling hands
- Excessive sleepiness
- Confusion or a feeling of disorientation
- Dark urine
- Abdominal pain
- Swelling of the abdomen, legs, ankles, or feet

Stages of Liver Damage

Liver failure occurs when a large portion of the liver becomes damaged beyond repair. Fibrosis, or scarring, is reversible in its early stages. Once the damage progresses to cirrhosis, it is difficult to treat and may develop into liver cancer.

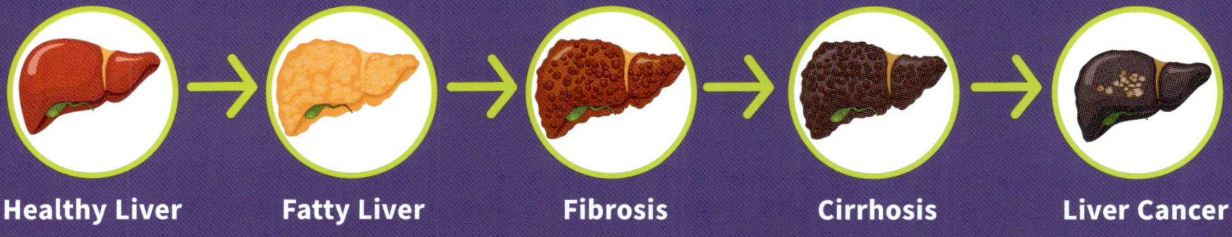

Medicine around the World

Diseases of the liver are a global health concern. Many hospitals, universities, and research centers around the world study the liver and develop treatments for the diseases that affect it. Several of these sites are renowned for their work in liver research, treatment, and transplants.

Mayo Clinic, United States

1

The Mayo Clinic is a world-renowned medical center with three different locations. It has campuses in Minnesota, Florida, and Arizona. The Mayo Clinic's Liver Transplant Program is one of the largest in the United States and among the best in the world. Its surgeons perform more than 500 liver transplants each year.

University of São Paulo, Brazil

2

The University of São Paulo is at the forefront of liver disease research in South America. Some of its main topics of research include viral hepatitis, cirrhosis, and autoimmune liver diseases. The university also promotes liver health awareness in the region.

Royal Free Hospital, United Kingdom

3

Based in London, the Sheila Sherlock Liver Centre at the Royal Free Hospital has an extensive liver transplant program. Professor Sheila Sherlock founded the liver unit in the 1950s. She is often called the "mother of hepatology" for her pioneering work in the field. Experts at the hospital perform about 100 liver transplants each year and train medical students from the University College London (UCL) Medical School.

University of Tokyo Hospital, Japan

4

Japan has one of the highest rates of liver cancer in the world. The country devotes significant resources to improving prevention, treatment, and early diagnosis of this disease. The University of Tokyo Hospital is known for its research into hepatitis and liver cancer.

What is a Hepatologist?

Doctors who specialize in treating liver conditions are called hepatologists. They diagnose and treat diseases that affect the rest of the biliary tract as well. Also known as the biliary tree, this is a network that includes the liver, gallbladder, bile ducts, and other structures that produce, store, or transport bile. Hepatologists also help patients manage existing liver conditions to prevent further damage. Specialists called transplant hepatologists focus on patients who need liver transplants. While this surgery is performed by a transplant surgeon, transplant hepatologists manage the complex care needed by a patient both before and after the operation.

Keeping the Liver Healthy

People can practice healthy habits to protect their livers. Nutrition, hydration, and exercise are very important. Vaccines are also available to prevent some liver diseases.

TIP 1

Eat a Balanced Diet
Fruits, vegetables, whole grains, and lean proteins support liver health. Foods high in fiber, such as leafy greens and whole grains, help the liver process fats efficiently.

TIP 2

Avoid Alcohol
Alcohol is one of the largest threats to the liver. Excessive alcohol consumption can lead to liver damage, such as fatty liver disease and cirrhosis.

TIP 3

Stay Hydrated
Drinking plenty of water helps the liver filter toxins and aids digestion.

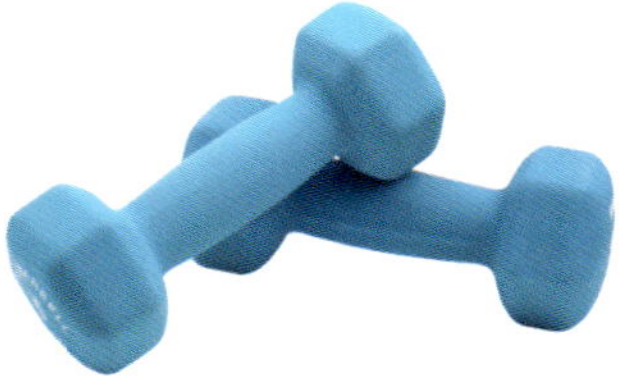

TIP 4

Exercise Regularly
Physical activity helps prevent fatty liver disease by regulating body weight and improving circulation.

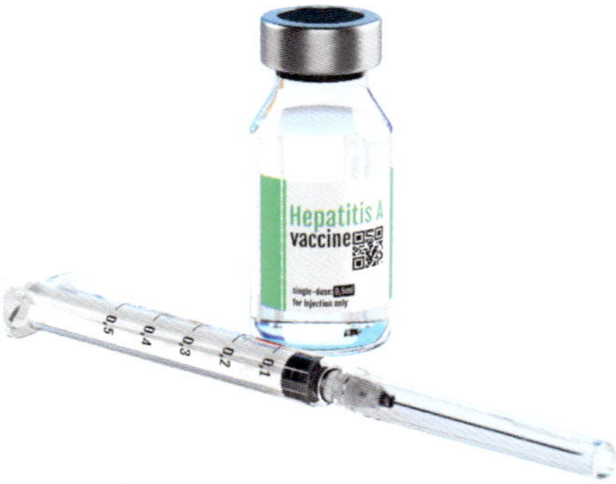

TIP 5

Get Vaccinated
Vaccines for hepatitis A and B help prevent these viral infections.

Activity: Build a Liver Model

The liver has a complex structure that includes lobes, blood vessels, and bile ducts. Try building a model to help you better understand the liver. Keep a diagram in front of you while making the model.

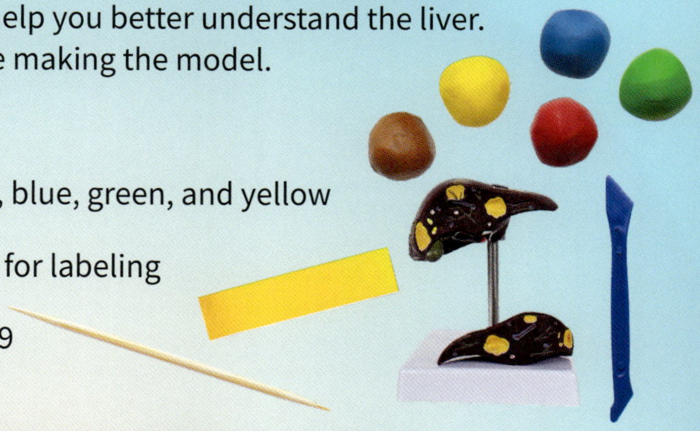

Materials

- Modeling clay in five colors: brown, red, blue, green, and yellow
- Plastic knife or sculpting tool
- Small labels or strips of paper and tape for labeling
- Toothpick
- Diagram of a liver, like the one on page 9

Steps

1. Create the Base Shape of the Liver: Using brown clay, shape a large, curved form that resembles a triangular wedge. The liver has a larger right lobe and a smaller left lobe, so remember to make the right side of your model bigger.

2. Define the Lobes: With your plastic knife, gently draw a line on the surface of the model to separate the right and left lobes of the liver. The line should not cut all the way through.

3. Add the Blood Vessels: Roll small pieces of red and blue clay to create thin, worm-like strands. Use red to represent the hepatic artery. Blue can represent the hepatic portal vein and hepatic vein.

4. Form the Bile Duct: Roll a small piece of green clay to create the bile duct. Position it near the blood vessels. It should extend toward the edge of the model.

5. Add Texture to Represent Hepatocytes: Gently press the surface of the liver with a toothpick to create a textured effect. The small dots or patterns represent the hepatocytes.

6. Label the Liver: Using the strips of paper or tape, write out small labels for each part of the liver. Include the right lobe, left lobe, hepatic artery, hepatic portal vein, hepatic vein, bile duct, hepatocytes, and anything else you can think of. Attach each label to the corresponding part of the model.

7. Display and Explain: Place your model on a table and review each part's function with your class or group. Explain how blood flows in and out. Discuss how bile moves through the bile duct for digestion.

Quiz

1

How many functions does the liver perform in the human body?

2

What are Kupffer cells?

3

What are the five vital organs?

4

Where is the liver located in the body?

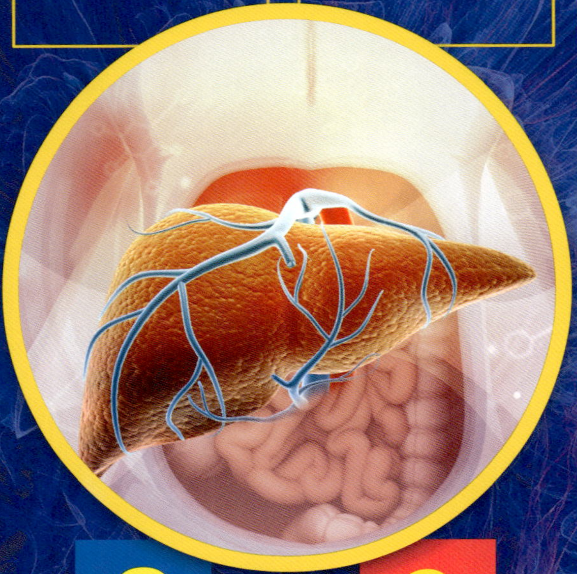

5

What are the three tubes of the portal triad?

6

Which hormone from the pancreas tells the liver to store excess glucose as glycogen?

7

Which organ stores the bile that the liver produces?

8

Can the liver regenerate?

9

Which ancient Greek physician suggested that the liver is the source of bile?

10

What is hepatitis?

ANSWERS

1. More than 500 **2.** Special immune cells in the liver **3.** The brain, heart, lungs, kidneys, and liver **4.** In the upper right abdomen, below the diaphragm and above the stomach, right kidney, and intestines **5.** Hepatic artery, hepatic portal vein, and bile duct **6.** Insulin **7.** The gallbladder **8.** Yes **9.** Hippocrates **10.** An inflammation of the liver

Key Words

abdomen: the part of the body that is located between the chest and pelvis and contains the digestive organs

autoimmune: relating to a condition where the immune system mistakenly attacks the body's own tissues

carbohydrates: nutrients found in foods such as bread, pasta, and rice

cells: the smallest structural and functional units of living organisms

digestive: related to breaking down food into smaller parts that the body can absorb

fatty acids: chemical compounds that make up fats and that the body can use to produce energy

glucose: a simple sugar that is the main energy source for the body's cells

hepatic: relating to the liver

homeostasis: the body's ability to maintain a stable internal environment despite external changes

hormones: chemical messengers that affect many functions in the body

inflammation: the body's response to injury or infection, often resulting in redness, swelling, heat, or pain

nutrients: substances found in food that provide energy for the body to use

organ: a distinct structure in the body that is made up of tissues and performs one or more specific functions

pathogens: microorganisms, such as bacteria or viruses, that cause diseases

proteins: nutrients found in foods such as meat, fish, and eggs

small intestine: a long, coiled tube in the abdomen where most digestion and absorption of nutrients occurs

toxins: poisonous substances

transplant: a medical procedure in which an organ or tissue is moved from one person to another, or from one part of the body to another

viral: relating to or caused by a virus, which is a type of microorganism that can infect cells and cause disease

Index

LIGHTBOX

SUPPLEMENTARY RESOURCES

Click on the plus icon ⊕ found in the bottom left corner of each spread to open additional teacher resources.

- Download and print the book's quizzes and activities
- Access curriculum correlations
- Explore additional web applications that enhance the Lightbox experience

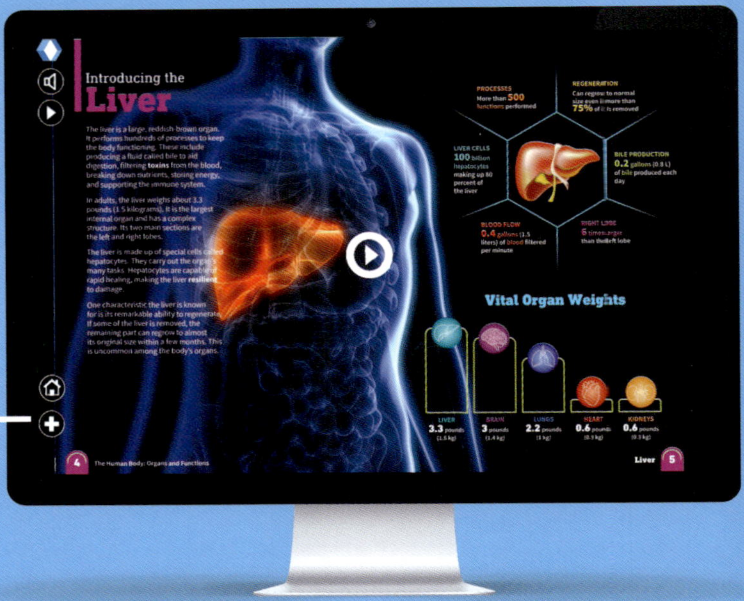

LIGHTBOX DIGITAL TITLES
Packed full of integrated media

VIDEOS

INTERACTIVE MAPS

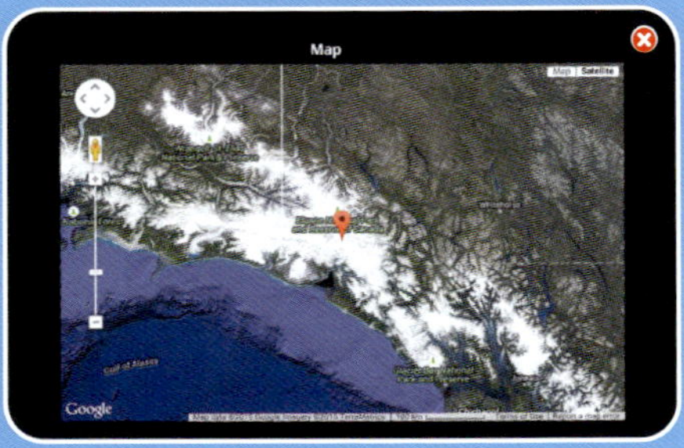

WEBLINKS

SLIDESHOWS

A cirque is a rounded, bowl-shaped area where snow collects.

QUIZZES

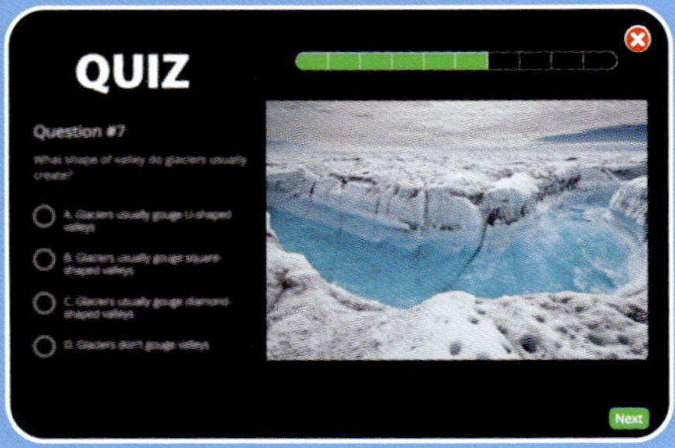

OPTIMIZED FOR

- ✓ TABLETS
- ✓ SMART BOARDS
- ✓ COMPUTERS
- ✓ AND MUCH MORE!

Published by Lightbox Learning Inc.
276 5th Avenue, Suite 704 #917
New York, NY 10001
Website: www.openlightbox.com

Library of Congress Control Number: 2025932678

ISBN 978-1-5105-8677-2 (hardcover)
ISBN 978-1-5105-8678-9 (static multi-user eBook)
ISBN 978-1-5105-8680-2 (interactive multi-user eBook)

Printed in Fargo, North Dakota, in the United States of America
2 3 4 5 6 7 8 9 0 30 29 28 27 26

012026
260119

Project Coordinator: Priyanka Das
Design: Jean Faye Rodriguez